introduction

Anytime
Anywhere
モバイル
あばりあみ

　道具を使わないテキスタイルは、場所に縛られることがないので、とても実用的だ。しかも手の中でおさまる道具なら、携帯でき、いつでも好きな時に始められる。日常の家事、子供の世話をしながら、ほんのわずかな合間に手を動かす。ラオスの女性は畑仕事の行き帰りに、歩きながらスピンドルで糸を紡いだ。英国シェットランド島の漁師の妻は、浜仕事の合間に、歩きながらでも編物が出来るよう腰に針を固定するベルトをつけてセーターを編んだ。ベドウィンの遊牧民は羊を追いながら糸を紡いだ。

　この"あばりあみ"で作れる物は伝統的な漁網や袋だけではない。今回この本では、袋も、服も、帽子もできることを紹介、「あばりあみ」の可能性を押し広げてくれた。

　道具をほとんど使わないことが原始的なのではない。たくさんの道具を必要とせず、携帯しながら物を作れることが、日常の雑事をこなす上で必要だったのだ。いつでもどこでも作れること、それが人の暮しの本来の姿なのではないだろうか。

　今回、新田恭子さんが紹介される「あばりあみ」は、その多くは漁師の網として使われてきた技法だという、それも世界各地でおこなわれてきたことに驚かされる。このポケットに入るだけの糸と針で、ここまで多様な物が出来ることに、私の中の原始の血が湧いてくる気がするのである。（本出）

SPINNUTS 2017

網をつくる道具・網針(あばり)

　「網針」(以下「あばり」と記す)は網をつくるために用いる道具です。網で漁をするところでは、国や時代も越えて用いられています。もちろん現代の日本でも、網を編む機会が少なくなってしまいましたが、破れた網の補修に使われて続けています。

　この「あばり」を用いて、色々な素材でつくるのが「フリースタイルあばりあみ」(以下「あばりあみ」と記す)です。つくりたいものの大きさやかたちを確認しながら、一目ずつ糸を結びます。それぞれの作り手の工夫を反映しやすく、制作意図や個性があらわれやすいところが魅力です。

"Netting-needles" are a tool for making fishnets, and have been used traditionally and worldwide wherever people catch fish with nets. In modern Japan, they are not used for making new nets so often anymore but are still needed for mending old

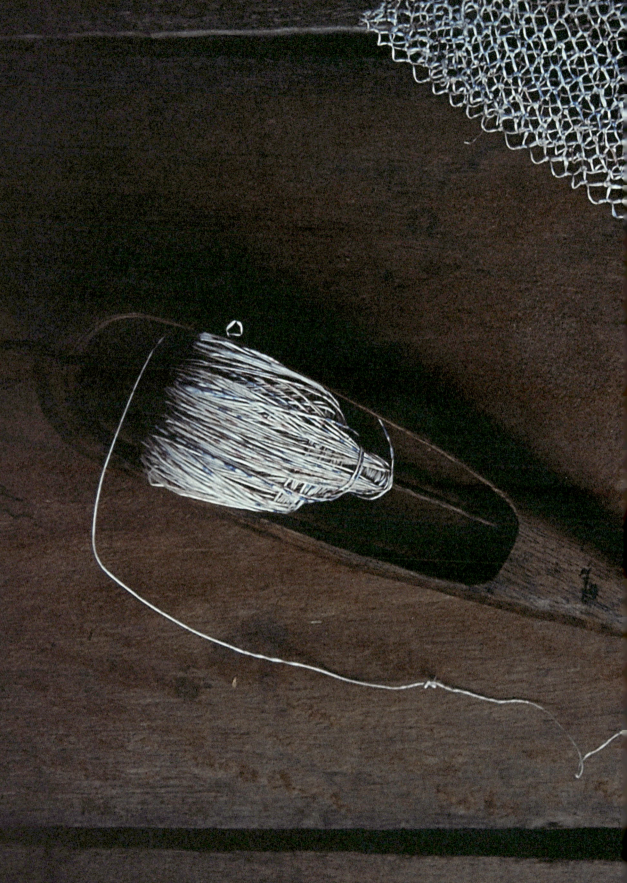

ラオス南部、川漁用の網をつくっています。細い竹ひごは、網の目を一定のサイズに統一するための道具として使われています。
A net for river fishery in southern Laos. The thin bamboo stick is used as a tool for keeping the mesh size even.

SPINNUTS ✳ スピナッツ・できるシリーズ 4

新田恭子の
フリースタイル
あばりあみ

Freestyle Fishnet Knotting
Kyoko NITTA

福島県いわき市小名浜港にある、巨大な「網大工」さんの仕事場では、遠洋漁業で使う大きな網をつくり、点検と修理もおこなっています。破れた網は、結び目が動かない特別な結び方で修理します。一番左で作業しているのは、「網大工」の棟梁さんです。
Fishnet makers in Onahama Port, Fukushima Prefecture produce, inspect and repair huge fishnets for distant water fishing. Torn nets are repaired in a special way with those knots completely fixed. Working on the left is the head fishnet maker.

ones and other purposes.
I've been advocating the "Freestyle Fishnet Knotting" for creating things with netting-needles and a variety of yarns. Once you learn a set of basic steps, you can work on your own creation by tying one knot after another while controlling its size and shape. What is good about this technique is each knotter can easily give some ingenuity to express their intent and uniqueness. With some yarn and a netting-needle at hand, you can make your own work anytime and anywhere.

網の「目（め）」について
本書では、網の隣り合う2つの結び目の間に渡っている糸とその内側の空間を「目」と呼びます。

About the term "mesh unit"

The span of yarn from a knot to the neighboring one is called "mesh unit" in this book.

SPINNUTS 2017 5

編み、網、結び
あばりあみ

　私が「あばり」を用いた網のつくり方をはじめて教わったのは、腰機の調査に訪れたラオスで、1999年のことでした。川で魚を捕るために、肥料袋を細長く切って撚りをかけた糸を、ひと目ひと目細かく「結び」ながら網をつくっていました。

　「編む」は、「セーターを編む」というように糸で何かをつくる技法を指すことが多い言葉ですが、本書で紹介している技法のことを「あばりあみ」と名付けた理由は、「あばり」という道具を用いること、そして漁網づくりに関連する技法だということが伝わりやすくするためです。「編み」と「網」の二つの意味を込めて、ひらがなで「あばりあみ」と表記することにしました。

　また、「編む」という言葉の示す範囲が大変広く、「あばりあみ」の動作を表わすには「編む」よりも「結ぶ」（英語ではknotting）という言葉がより正確なため、本書では技法のことを「あばりあみ」、ひとつひとつの動作を「結ぶ」と表記することにし、「あばりあみ」の英語訳は「Freestyle Fishnet Knotting」としました。

What's Freestyle Fishnet Knotting ?

It was while researching backstrap looms in Laos in 1999 that I first learned this knotting technique. I happened to see a local fisherman making a fine fishnet with twisted yarns made from a fertilizer bag. The technique featured in this book is about making knots with netting-needles, and has been passed on among fishnet makers. In this book, I call it "freestyle fishnet knotting" when it is applied to other purposes including artistic expressions.

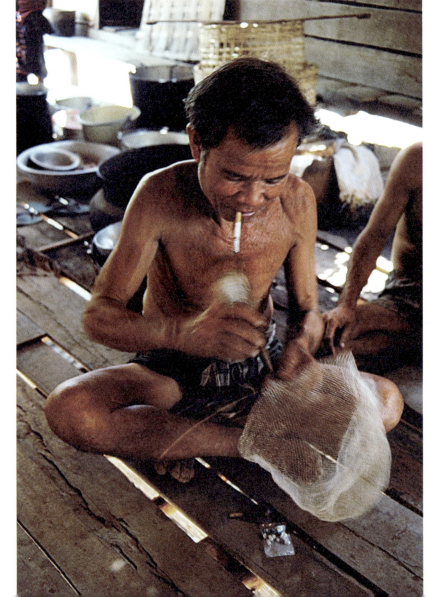

ラオス南部で網のつくりかたを教わった男性です。私は「ラオスの師匠」と呼んでいます。
This is my Laotian master teacher, who gave me net-making lessons in southern Laos.

三重県鳥羽市の「海の博物館」に展示されているガラス製浮玉「びんだま」。左右共に同じ結び方ですが、表に出る面が違います。
These glass fishing floats are shown in Toba Sea-folk Museum in Mie Prefecture. The two front floats are wrapped with nets — one showing "front side" while the other showing "reverse" — but both are made with the same knotting technique.

市の「ぎやまん師匠」吉田榮作氏（右側）
my master-teacher-in-Iwaki Eisaku Yoshida

イスティングスの「漁師博物館」にも、ガラス製「あばり」の展示がありました。
astings Fishermen's Museum in the U.K. glass fishing floats and netting-needles.

　世界中で「あばり」は使い続けられています。人類が網をつくりはじめた遥かな昔から今日まで、ずっと使い続けられているのではないでしょうか。

　「あばり」を使った網のつくり方は、地域や漁の方法により多数あります。私がラオスで習った方法は、日本ではガラス製浮玉（いわき市では「ぎやまん」と呼びます）をロープで包む結び方と同じだということを、遠洋漁業の漁船で働いていた福島県いわき市在住の元漁師、吉田榮作氏に教わりました。この方法だと結び目が動くので、球をぴったり包むのに最適です。結び目を重ねて形をつくるので、気に入った形ができたところで終わりにしてしまっても、構造上の問題はありません。

　現在の日本では、「あばり」は漁港でしか見かけられなくなってきています。漁港でも、工場で大量生産された網を買って加工する時代になっているので、「あばり」の出番は以前より減ってきているようです。

　「あばり」を使った、こんなに単純で自由度の高い技法を途絶えさせてしまうことは、人類にとって大きな損失であると思っています。

Netting-needles are used around the world. I guess people have kept using this tool since far distant past when our ancestors made early nets.
Ways for making nets with a netting-needle vary with regions and fishing methods. Mr. Eisaku Yoshida, who used to work on tuna fishing boats and lives in Iwaki, Fukushima Prefecture, points out that the way I learned in Laos is the same with how they tie knots for making such nets to wrap and fix glass fishing floats onto ropes. This way is suitable for wrapping something spherical as the knots' positions are adjustable. You can finish at any point where you think you've got a right shape. Finishing anywhere won't change the net's basic structure.
In modern Japan, you can hardly find netting-needles outside fishing communities, even where factory-made nets prevail and making netting-needles obsolete.
Failing to inherit this simple but highly flexible technique would mean a serious loss for human culture.

SPINNUTS 2017　7

お好きな「あばり」で

　「あばり」は漁網屋さん、釣具屋さんなどで売っています。インターネット上でも販売されています。自分の手に馴染む「あばり」を手づくりすることもできます。

　竹、木材、プラスティックなど、いろいろな素材を使った、さまざまなサイズの「あばり」があります。初心者の方には、握りやすい5号くらい（長さ20cm、幅3cm程度）の大きさのものが使いやすいと思います。「あばり」の大きさは、「あばりあみ」では網の目の大きさに影響しません。

　毛糸などをできるだけ切らずに使いたい場合は、もっと大きな「あばり」を用いるのも、ひとつの方法です。

About netting-needles

You can get netting-needles at fishing gear shops or online. You can also make ones by hand so that they would fit your hands or purpose.
Netting-needles, made of various materials including bamboo, wood and plastic, come in different sizes. Beginners often find size 5's netting-needle (about 20cm long and 3cm wide) easy to hold. Note that the size of the needle has nothing to do with the mesh size you'll make.
In case you want to use a long length of yarn without cutting and connecting, use a netting-needle big enough to load the whole yarn.

張りのある糸が向いています

　「あばりあみ」には、張りのある糸が向いています。初心者の方には、「結びコード」（※19ページ参照）の金色と銀色の糸をおすすめします。結びやすいだけでなく、ほどきやすいことがその理由です。他にも、撚りがしっかりかかっている麻糸（ヘンプ、リネン、ジュート、苧麻など）もおすすめです。また、テープヤーンも向いています。この糸は結びやすいのですが、ほどきにくいので初心者の方は注意しましょう。

　向いていないのは、張りのない糸（カシミヤなどの柔らかすぎる糸やファンシー・ヤーンなど）です。

Resilient yarns are suitable

Resilient yarns are suitable for freestyle fishnet knotting. Beginners would find it easier to handle such yarns for decorative knots — gold or silver ones are especially recommended. They are easy not only to knot but also to undo. Also, strongly twisted yarns including hemp, flax and ramie are easy to tie and untie knots as well. Tape yarns are also easy to make knots, but are not so when you undo them.
On the other hand, vulnerable yarns like soft cashmere yarns and fancy yarns are not suitable for freestyle fishnet knotting.

右利き用 基本動作
FOR RIGHT-HANDERS

■「あばり」に糸を巻きとりましょう

1 左手親指で糸端を押さえる。
2 親指より先の糸にゆとりを持たせて、「あばり」の中央の棒に糸をかける。
3 糸を「あばり」の下部に当て、「あばり」を裏返す。
4 左手親指で糸を押さえて、糸を「あばり」の中央の棒にかける。
5 糸を「あばり」の下部に当てて、「あばり」を裏返す。
6 2〜5を繰り返す。中央の棒が糸で覆われてしまうまで、巻き取れます。

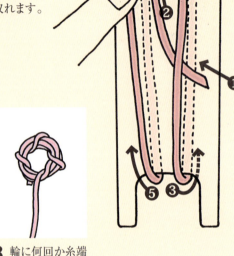

■「最初の輪」をつくりましょう

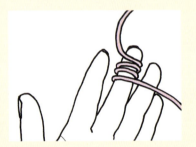  

1 糸端を10cmくらい残して、左手中指に糸を3回巻きつけ、糸の輪をつくる。
2 糸の輪から中指を抜き、糸端を輪に巻きつける。
3 輪に何回か糸端を巻きつけ、輪を安定させる。

■「あばりあみ」をしましょう

結び目はひとつずつ力を入れて引き締めると、全体の形が安定します。つくりたいものによって、目の大小を調節したり、大きさをそろえたり、逆にふぞろいにしたり、だんだん大きく、またはだんだん小さくするなどの工夫ができます。

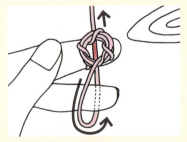 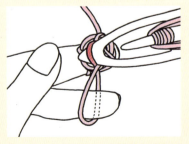 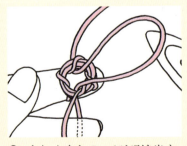

1 図のように糸を中指に掛け、輪の後ろに糸をはさむ。
2 糸の赤くなっている部分を「あばり」の先ですくう。
3 すくった糸を、5cmほど引き出す。

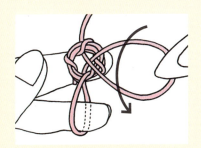

4 引き出した糸の輪を、時計と逆方向に半回転させる。

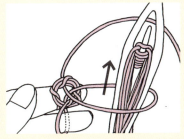

5 糸の輪の下側から上に向かって「あばり」を通す。

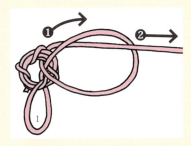

6 ❶方向へ引き、中指が入っていた輪の大きさを調節。そして❷方向に引き、結び目を締める。

7 「最初の輪」に「最初のひと目」を結んだ様子。

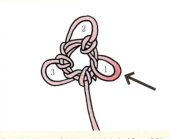

8 「最初の輪」に3目以上結んだら、「最初のひと目」に糸を結ぶ。

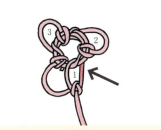

9 平らな円状につくりたい場合は、「最初のひと目」にもう一度糸を結んで増やし目をする。

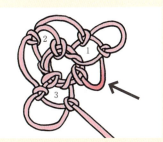

10 様子を見て、増やし目をしながら、結び進める。

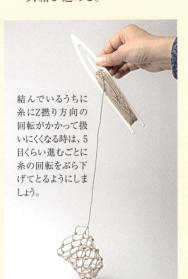

結んでいるうちに糸にZ撚り方向の回転がかかって扱いにくくなる時は、5目くらい進むごとに糸の回転をぶら下げてとるようにしましょう。

Load up a yarn onto the netting-needle. (for right-handers)

① Hold the yarn's end with your left thumb.
② Hang the yarn onto the needle's center post/tongue, giving some latitude between your thumb and the post.
③ Put the yarn onto the needle's bottom (between the two fins), and flip the needle over.
④ Hold the yarn's end with your left thumb as shown graphically, and hang it on the center post.
⑤ Put the yarn onto the needle's bottom, and flip the needle over.
⑥ Repeat the process ②〜⑤. You can load the yarn till the needle's center post is full.

Make a starter loop. (for right-handers)

① Make a triple loop by coiling the yarn around your left middle finger, leaving 10cm of the yarn's end uncoiled.
② Take the finger off, and put the yarn's end around the loop.
③ Twist the yarn end around several times till the loop gets steady.

Work on your net. (for right-handers)

The whole shape gets steady when you tie each knot firmly. Take a right strategy for your purpose; many different yarns of different thickness and materials are available while you can choose what mesh size you like, making it even, uneven, narrowing or widening.

① Put your left index finger under a point (towards the bottom right) where you intend to make a knot. Put the yarn away through between your left middle finger and the point.
② Hitch the yarn's part (shown as shaded in the graphic).
③ Pull it out 5cm.
④ Give a half anticlockwise turn to the loop of the drawn cord.
⑤ Pass the netting-needle through the loop upwards from the bottom.
⑥ Pull the yarn in the direction of the arrow ❶, and then fix the size of the loop that was around your middle finger earlier. Then, pull the yarn in the direction of arrow ❷ to tighten the knot.
⑦ The graphic shows the state after the first mesh unit is made.
⑧ When 3 or more mesh units are done, tie the yarn to the first mesh unit.
⑨ If you plan to make a flat and circular piece, increase a knot by tying the yarn to it again.
⑩ See how it develops, and increase another knot or more if necessary.
Let the unfinished piece down every 5 knots when you need to undo an increasing counterclockwise twist in the yarn.

左利き用 基本動作
FOR LEFT-HANDERS

■「あばり」に糸を巻きとりましょう

1 右手親指で糸端を押さえる。
2 親指より先の糸にゆとりを持たせて、「あばり」の中央の棒に糸をかける。
3 糸を「あばり」の下部に当て、「あばり」を裏返す。
4 右手親指で糸を押さえて、糸を「あばり」の中央の棒にかける。
5 糸を「あばり」の下部に当てて、「あばり」を裏返す。
6 2〜5を繰り返す。中央の棒が糸で覆われてしまうまで、巻き取れます。

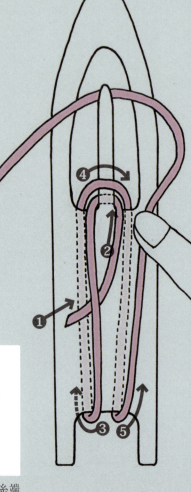

■「最初の輪」をつくりましょう

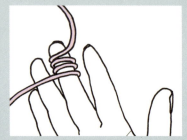  

1 糸端を10cmくらい残して、右手中指に糸を3回巻きつけ、糸の輪をつくる。
2 糸の輪から中指を抜き、糸端を輪に巻きつける。
3 輪に何回か糸端を巻きつけ、輪を安定させる。

■「あばりあみ」をしましょう

結び目はひとつずつ力を入れて引き締めると、全体の形が安定します。つくりたいものによって、目の大小を調節したり、大きさをそろえたり、逆にふぞろいにしたり、だんだん大きく、またはだんだん小さくするなどの工夫ができます。

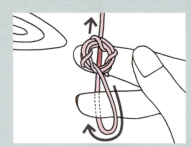 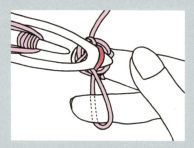 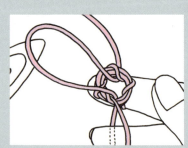

1 図のように糸を中指に掛け、輪の後ろに糸をはさむ。
2 糸の赤くなっている部分を「あばり」の先ですくう。
3 すくった糸を、5cmほど引き出す。

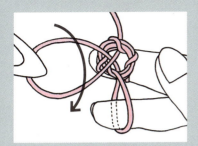

4 引き出した糸の輪を、時計の方向に半回転させる。

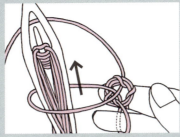

5 糸の輪の下側から上に向かって「あばり」を通す。

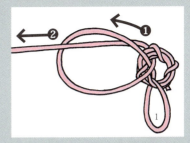

6 ❶方向へ引き、中指が入っていた輪の大きさを調節。そして❷方向に引き、結び目を締める。

7 「最初の輪」に「最初のひと目」を結んだ様子。

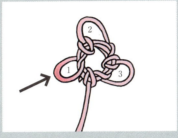

8 「最初の輪」に3目以上結んだら、「最初のひと目」に糸を結ぶ。

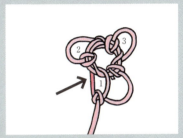

9 平らな円状につくりたい場合は、「最初のひと目」にもう一度糸を結んで増やし目をする。

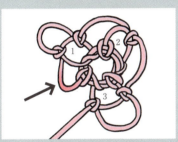

10 様子を見て、増やし目をしながら、結び進める。

結んでいるうちに糸にS撚り方向の回転がかかって扱いにくくなる時は、5目くらい進むごとに糸の回転をぶら下げてとるようにしましょう。

Load up a yarn onto the netting-needle. (for left-handers)

① Hold the yarn's end with your right thumb.
② Hang the yarn onto the needle's center post/tongue, giving some latitude between your thumb and the post.
③ Put the yarn onto the needle's bottom (between the two fins), and flip the needle over.
④ Hold the yarn's end with your right thumb as shown graphically, and hang it on the center post.
⑤ Put the yarn onto the needle's bottom, and flip the needle over.
Repeat the process ②~⑤. You can load the yarn till the needle's center post is full.

Make a starter loop. (for left-handers)

① Make a triple loop by coiling the yarn around your right middle finger, leaving 10cm of the yarn's end uncoiled.
② Take the finger off, and put the yarn's end around the loop.
③ Twist the yarn end around several times till the loop gets steady.

Work on your net. (for left-handers)

The whole shape gets steady when you tie each knot firmly. Take a right strategy for your purpose; many different yarns of different thickness and materials are available while you can choose what mesh size you like, making it even, uneven, narrowing or widening.

① Put your right index finger under a point (towards the bottom right) where you intend to make a knot. Put the yarn away through between your middle finger and the point.
② Hitch the yarn's part (shown as shaded in the graphic).
③ Pull it out 5cm.
④ Give a half clockwise turn to the loop of the drawn cord.
⑤ Pass the netting-needle through the loop upwards from the bottom.
⑥ Pull the yarn in the direction of the arrow ❶, and then fix the size of the loop that was around your middle finger earlier. Then, pull the yarn in the direction of arrow ❷ to tighten the knot.
⑦ The graphic shows the state after the first mesh unit is made.
⑧ When 3 or more mesh units are done, tie the yarn to the first mesh unit.
⑨ If you plan to make a flat and circular piece, increase a knot by tying the yarn to it again.
⑩ See how it develops, and increase another knot or more if necessary.
Let the unfinished piece down every 5 knots when you need to undo an increasing clockwise twist in the yarn.

増やし目と減らし目 Increasing and decreasing knots

完成させたい形をイメージしながら、必要な所で増やし目、減らし目を入れましょう。
Form the intending shape by increasing and decreasing knots.

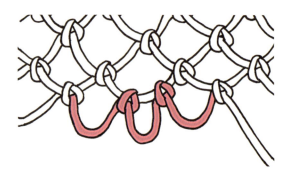

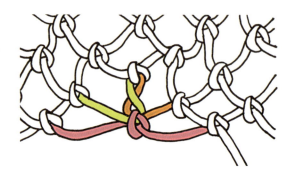

増やし目

ひとつの目に2回糸を結ぶと、増やし目になります。
Increasing knots means you tie two knots in one unit of mesh.

減らし目

となり合う2つの目を重ねて糸を結ぶと、減らし目になります。
Decreasing knots means you tie one knot with two adjacent units of mesh put together.

植物のかたちを参考に　*column*

「あばりあみ」には、棒針編みやかぎ針編みのような編み図はありません。増やし目や減らし目は、完成させたいかたちや大きさになるように、全体の様子を見ながら入れる所を決めます。私が平らな円をつくるときに参考にしているのは、ひまわりの花の中心部や種のつき方です。松ぼっくりは小さな袋物をつくる時のヒントになることでしょう。ひまわりや松ぼっくりをよく見ると、右向きと左向きのらせんが見えてきます。数学の本によると、らせんの本数にフィボナッチ数列の数が現れるのだそうですが、難しいことは気にせず、作業を進めてください。もし、期待していたかたちと少し違うように思えても、結び目は強く引っ張ると動くため、かたちを整えることができるはずです。作業を終わりたい所で終えることができて、終えた後も足したい所に自由にあみを足せるフレキシブルさも、「あばりあみ」の大きな魅力です。

Use shapes of plants as reference.

"Freestyle fishnet knotting", unlike needle knitting and crocheting, doesn't use patterns. You can form a piece into the shape and size intended by increasing or decreasing knots at proper points. I often refer to sunflowers' head inflorescence, especially how the seeds are arranged, when knotting and shaping a flat circle. You can also learn from pine cones when you plan to make a small bag. Take a close look at a sunflower or a pine cone, and you'll notice clockwise and anti-clockwise spirals there. Some mathematical sources say consecutive Fibonacci numbers appear in such spiral arrangements. Well, keep on knotting with mathematics left behind. Don't worry even when the shape gets somewhat wrong. You can move and adjust positions of those tied knots so that the whole piece looks right.

糸つなぎと糸しまつ Finishing off a yarn end and adding another yarn

木の葉を隠すなら森へ、という言葉にならって、糸端は目立たないように、2～4回ほど網の目に結んでから短く切ると、たくさん結び目があるなかにまぎれて目立ちにくくなります。

Someone in a story said, "Where does a wise man hide a leaf? In the forest." You can also make your yarn's end disappear among other knots by cutting the end close after tying a few knots.

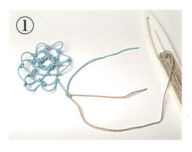
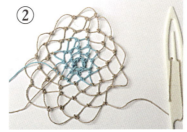
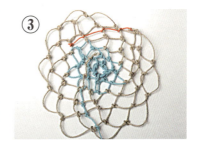

糸つなぎ

「あばり」に巻いた糸が無くなったら、空になった「あばり」に新たな糸を巻き取り、図①のように糸端を結び合わせます。解けにくければ、どんな結び方でも問題ありません。図②のように網をつくり続けた後に、図③のようにしまつします。

When the yarn loaded onto the needle gets used up, you can reload the empty needle with another yarn. Tie to connect the two yarns' ends (see ①), and then start working on your net again (see ②). You can tie it in whatever way if the knot is firm.

糸しまつ

結び終わりは図③のオレンジ色の糸のように、糸端を2～4回以上、糸に少しゆとりをもたせながら結んでから短く切ります。

Cut the end close after tying a few or more knots while giving some latitude to the yarn (shown in orange) not to distort the whole shape (see ③).

初心者向けの「最初の輪」と「最初のひと目」
Tips for beginners: how to make an initial knot

初心者の方は、「あばり」と糸に加えて、直径1～3cm程度の小さな輪を使うと結びやすくなります。革や厚めのフェルトから切り出してもいいですし、モールを輪にしたもの、市販のプラスチックの輪などがおすすめです。糸端を8cmくらい残して、10～13ページの方法で輪に直接糸を結びます。1周に3目以上結びます。

Beginners might find 1-3 cm diameter rings useful as a starter loop. You can make ones by cutting out from a leather sheet or a thick felt piece or by looping an ornamental steel wire. Such rings made of plastic or something can be found and bought at stores. As shown on pages 10 and 13, tie the yarn directly to a starter loop three times or more, leaving 8 cm as margin.

ボトルを入れる袋をつくりましょう
Won't you make a bottle bag?

ボトルがちょうど入るサイズの網の袋をつくりましょう。しっかりと撚りのかかった麻糸やもめん糸、太めのコードなどの丈夫な糸が向いています。結び目が動くので、同じくらいの大きさの違う形のびんも入れられます。ペットボトルのサイズでつくると、ペットボトルホルダーにもなりますよ。

1 増やし目をしながら、びんの底と同じサイズの円をつくる。

2 結び続けて側面をつくる。

3 引っ張って様子を見ながら、びんの口まで側面をつくる。

4 2目結んでひっくり返す。これを何度かくり返して、取っ手をつくる。

5 取っ手をつくり終えた糸を、本体の端に結ぶ。

6 取っ手の端に糸を結ぶ。

7 5と6をくり返して取っ手をつけ終えたら、15cmほど残して糸を切る。

8 糸のしまつをする。

9 完成。

スヌードをつくりましょう
You can make snoods.

張りのある毛糸やモヘア糸が向いています。写真のスヌードは甘より単糸の毛糸を45g使いました。ファンシー・ヤーンなどの柔らかい糸を使いたい場合は、張りのある糸と引きそろえると結びやすくなるので、おすすめです。完成品は網の目によって全体がよく伸び、結び目も動くので、巻いた時の収まりがよく、ターバンなどにも使えます。また、ベストにも応用できます。

1 直径5cmの円をつくる。

2 ひっくり返して半周分結ぶ。

3 ひっくり返してさらに半周分結ぶ。（写真は2目結んだ様子）

4 2と3をくり返してスヌードの幅の広さまで楕円形を広げる。

5 1段結ぶたびにひっくり返して、結び進める。

6 必要な長さまで続ける。

7 編み始めと結び合せる。

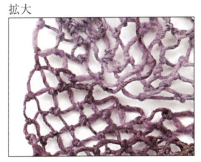

拡大

8 完成。

工程写真：新田恭子　イラスト：ひとえ

楽しく使える「あばりあみ」の作品

太めの糸でざくざくつくると、あっという間に完成します。細い糸の網も繊細でいいものです。革紐、麻糸、テープヤーン、リボン、細いワイヤー、毛糸などが使えます。何本かの糸を引き揃えたり、ビーズやスパンコールを糸に通してから「あばり」に巻き取ってつくったり、糸を変えるだけで、表情が大きく変わります。網の構造によって伸縮性をもったり、糸にかかる回転によって全体のかたちが変形したりと、手の中でひと目ひと目結びながら、まるで糸でできた結晶の様に変化してゆく網のかたちを観察する面白さも格別です。

Pieces out of netting-needlework are fun to use.

You can finish your work so quickly if you use thicker yarns and make the mesh size bigger. On the other hand, you can do a subtle job with a finer count of yarns. You can choose from a variety of materials including leather cord, woolen yarn, tape yarn, ribbon, thin wire and wool. You can also give big changes by threading a yarn through beads or spangles or using some different yarns for the same piece. Pieces with the network structure are stretchy, and their whole shapes are influenced by intensity of the thread's twist. Enjoy viewing how the net's shape changes as your netting-needlework goes on.

あとがき

　あばりあみは、糸を結ぶことができる人なら誰でもとりくめます。様々な状況下におられる、たくさんの方々に楽しんでいただくことを願いながら普及活動をすすめ、同時に私自身の作品も制作しています。

　あばりあみの魅力を教えてくれたラオスの師匠、吉田榮作ぎやまん師匠、あばりあみでつくった作品の発表やワークショップでお世話になっているギャラリーギャラリーの川嶋啓子さん、スピナッツ出版の本出ますみさん、英語監修をしていただいたGlen Kaufmanさん、翻訳を引き受けてくれた夫の高島正仲をはじめ、これまでにお力をかしていただいた多くの恩人と共に、あばりあみに関心を寄せてくださっている皆様に、心より感謝の意を表します。

Afterword

Freestyle Fishnet Knotting is for anyone knowing how to tie knots. Once you grasp its basics, your hands will learn to work by themselves. I produce my own work while trying to invite more people from various backgrounds to enjoy this technique.
My big and sincere thank-you goes to my Laotian master teacher who showed me how this technique is fascinating; another master teacher Eisaku Yoshida; Keiko Kawashima of GalleryGallery who let my exhibitions and workshops happen; Masumi Honde of SPINNUTS Publications who kindly published this leaflet; Glen Kaufman who supervised the English wording; Masanaka Takashima who translated the passage into English; many other supporters of Freestyle Fishnet Knotting.

■ 新田 恭子（にった きょうこ）　Kyoko NITTA
繊維造形作家、フリースタイルあばりあみ主宰、大学非常勤講師。1990年、京都市立芸術大学美術学部工芸科染織専攻 卒業。1992年、中国貴州民族学院留学修了。1993年、京都市立芸術大学大学院美術研究科工芸専攻（染織）修士課程 修了。京都にあるギャラリーギャラリーを中心に、個展と企画展などで「あばり」を使って制作した作品を多数発表中。
Kyoko NITTA shows her art works made with netting-needles at Kyoto's GalleryGallery and other locations.
＜ウェブサイト＞ nitta-knotter.com

※表紙写真での使用糸「結びコード」はタカギ繊維の商品です。
　タカギ繊維　京都府京都市上京区黒門通上長者町上る榎町347-2　TEL 075-441-4181

「光」（部分）2013　撮影：矢野誠

スピナッツ 別冊 スピナッツできるシリーズ4 新田恭子のフリースタイルあばりあみ Freestyle Fishnet Knotting Kyoko NITTA	初　版　2017年1月17日 第2版第2刷　2018年9月20日 編　集　スピナッツ出版 発 行 所　スピナッツ	住　　所　京都市北区等持院南町46-6 T E L　075-462-5966 F A X　075-461-2450 M A I L　office@spinnuts.kyoto.jp U R L　www.spinnuts.kyoto.jp
	文　　新田恭子・本出ますみ イラスト　新田恭子 翻　訳　高島正仲	
Freestyle Fishnet Knotting Kyoko NITTA		Printed in Japan
January 2017 (first edition, first printing) September 2017 (second edition, first printing)	Publisher SPINNUTS Publications 46-6 Tojiin Minamimachi, Kitaku, Kyoto, Japan www.spinnuts.kyoto.jp	Copyright© 2017 SPINNUTS Publications All rights reserved. No part of this publication may be reproduced, stored in a retrieval system or transmitted, by any means, electronic, mechanical, photocopying, recording or otherwise without the prior written permission of the publisher.
※本誌の内容を転載される場合は、必ず編集部までご連絡ください。	Text and Illustration by Kyoko Nitta Editing and Introduction in Japanese by Masumi Honde of SPINNUTS Publications Translation by Masanaka Takashima